SIMPLY SOUND

Science Adventures with Jasper the Origami Bat

TWANG!

by Eric Braun

illustrated by Jamey Christoph

PICTURE WINDOW BOOKS
a capstone imprint

Everyone says Heather is loud, even her mom.

One day, instead of doing her homework, Heather made cool stuff with her science notes. She made a paper bat and named it Jasper. She made Jasper make loud noises too.

SQUEAK
SQUEAK
SQUEAK

"My goodness. Why don't you take a break from that racket and help me?"

YES!

3

POP!

BANG!

CLANG!

"Whoa! That girl is loud. My wings are vibrating."

"How can a sound shake your wings? It's just sound."

Jasper knew a lot about sound. "Sound is made of waves that travel through the air," he said to Jim the dog. "Tiny things move when strong waves hit them."

4

BAM!

*CLINK!

"Watch this."

As Heather banged the pot and pan, the sprinkles bounced on the paper.

"Cool!"

CRASH!

"Bats are really good at **hearing** and **feeling sounds**. That's why all of this noise is **so annoying!**"

"Dogs hear well too. Let's get out of here."

"Do you want to learn more about **sound?**" Jasper asked. He looped a rubber band around the doorknob and pulled it tight.

"**Not if it's loud,**" Jim said.

"Don't worry. Use your paw to pluck this band."

TWANG!

"That sound is caused by the rubber band moving back and forth really quickly. That motion is called **vibration**. When something vibrates, it makes waves in the air."

Next Jasper pulled the rubber band even tighter. "Pluck it now," he grunted.

PING!

"It sounds higher."

"Right," Jasper said. "Pitch is how high or low a sound is. This time you got a higher pitch because the rubber band vibrated faster."

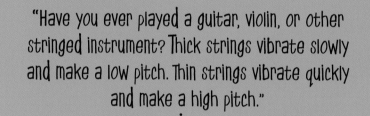

"Have you ever played a guitar, violin, or other stringed instrument? Thick strings vibrate slowly and make a low pitch. Thin strings vibrate quickly and make a high pitch."

"Well, I don't play stringed instruments. I'm a dog! And you can't tell me that every sound is made by vibrations. When people talk nothing vibrates."

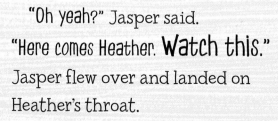

"Oh yeah?" Jasper said. "Here comes Heather. **Watch this.**" Jasper flew over and landed on Heather's throat.

I CAN'T FIND MY BAT!

NOTHING IS GOOD ON TV!

LET ME KNOW WHEN THE COOKIES ARE DONE!

Jim could tell Jasper was vibrating—a lot!

"Whoa! I can almost feel a vibration from here."

Heather swiped Jasper off her throat and ran for the door.

"Hey, what's that outside?"

"Off she goes!"

"See?" Jasper said. **"All sound is vibration.** Inside a person's throat are **vocal cords** that vibrate to make a voice."

"You said vibrations make waves," Jim said. "How does that happen?"

"Easy. Air is made up of tiny **molecules.** When an object vibrates, it pushes air molecules around it. Those molecules bump into the molecules next to them, and those molecules move. And so on. This is a wave of air molecules. We can't see it, but we can hear it."

This got Jim thinking.

"How does hearing work?"

"Well, sound waves travel away from the source in all directions," said Jasper.

"And an ear catches them?" asked Jim.

OUTER EAR

EARDRUM

NERVE

EAR CANAL

COCHLEA

BONES

"That's right. The **outer ear** catches the sound waves. The **ear canal** funnels the waves to the **eardrum**. The waves make the eardrum vibrate. Tiny bones then transfer vibrations to the **cochlea**. Then the vibrations are sent to a **nerve**. Finally, the nerve sends the message to the **brain**, and you hear **sound**."

"Some animals, such as bats and dogs, have really big ears so they can collect a lot of sound waves."

"Yep. My ears are pretty big."

"Bats collect vibrations for echolocation. It's how we fly or find food when it's too dark to see. We make a very high-pitched noise. If the sound waves bounce back to us, we know something is in the way. Then we fly around it or eat it."

"That's awesome," Jim said. "Speaking of sounds, I think I hear someone coming!"

17

"You were right," Jasper said. "There's Heather's mom. And she might be on to us."

"Why is she cupping her ear with her hand?"

"It's like she's making her outer ear bigger—so she can hear us better."

"We better be quiet."

VA-ROOM

BEEP!

HONK!

"SO, Heather's mom can hear us because **sound waves travel in all directions.** How come we don't hear sounds from all around the world all the time?"

"As sound travels, it spreads out and gets weaker. It also can bounce back if it hits a barrier like a wall or mountain. **Some barriers absorb the sound,** so it just stops."

19

GLOSSARY

cochlea—a spiral-shaped part of the ear that helps send sound messages to the brain

ear canal—a tube-shaped part of the ear that funnels vibrations to the eardrum

eardrum—a thin piece of skin stretched tight like a drum inside the ear; the eardrum vibrates when sound waves strike it

echolocation—the process of using sounds and echoes to locate objects; bats use echolocation to find food

molecule—the atoms making up the smallest part of a substance

nerve—a thin fiber that carries messages between the brain and other parts of the body

outer ear—the part of the ear on the outside of the body

pitch—how high or low a sound is

source—the place where something begins

vibrate—to move back and forth quickly

vocal cords—bands of skin in a person's air pipe; vocal cords vibrate and make sound

wave—a vibration of sound that travels through the air, water, or something else

READ MORE

Goldsmith, Mike. *Discover Science: Light and Sound.* London: Kingfisher, 2012.

Royston, Angela. *Sound and Hearing.* My World of Science. Chicago: Heinemann Library, 2008.

Winnick, Nick. *Hearing.* World of Wonder. New York: Weigl Publishers, 2010.

MAKE AN ORIGAMI BAT

Jasper is a pretty awesome little bat. Check out these instructions to make your very own origami bat!

what you need

origami paper

WHAT YOU DO

Folds

Valley folds are shown with a dashed line. One side of the paper is folded against the other like a book. A sharp fold is made by running your finger along the fold line.

Mountain folds are shown with a white or pink dashed and dotted line. The paper should be folded sharply behind the model.

Arrows

single-pointed arrow: Fold the paper in the direction of the arrow.

double-pointed arrow: Fold the paper and then unfold it.

half-pointed arrow: Fold the paper behind.

1. Start with the colored side of the paper face down. Valley fold the bottom corner to the top corner.

2. Valley fold the right corner to the left corner and unfold.

3. Valley fold both bottom points to the top point, creating a square.

22

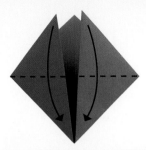

4. Valley fold the top layer of the two top points to meet the bottom point.

5. Valley fold the two middle points to meet with both the left and right edges.

6. Turn over the model.

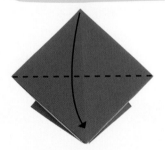

7. Valley fold the top point to the bottom point.

8. Make a valley fold with the two top layers of the bottom point, about 3/4 inch (1.9 cm) from the top edge.

9. Mountain fold the top point.

10. Valley fold the side points so they meet at the center line of the model.

11. Unfold the model's "wings."

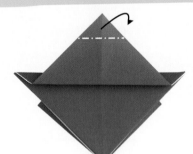

INDEX

more books in the series:

Diggin' Dirt: Science Adventures with Kitanai the Origami Dog

Glowing with Electricity: Science Adventures with Glenda the Origami Firefly

Lookin' for Light: Science Adventures with Manny the Origami Moth

Wild Weather: Science Adventures with Sonny the Origami Bird

Thanks to our advisers for their expertise, research, and advice:
Paul Ohmann, PhD, Associate Professor and Chair of Physics
University of St. Thomas, St. Paul, Minnesota

Terry Flaherty, PhD, Professor of English
Minnesota State University, Mankato

Editor: Shelly Lyons
Designer: Ashlee Suker
Art Director: Nathan Gassman
Production Specialist: Eric Manske
The illustrations in this book were created digitally.

Picture Window Books are published by Capstone,
1710 Roe Crest Drive, North Mankato, Minnesota 56003
www.capstonepub.com

Library of Congress Cataloging-in-Publication Data
Braun, Eric, 1971- author.
Simply sound : science adventures with Jasper the origami
bat / by Eric Braun.
pages cm. — (Nonfiction picture books. Origami
science adventures)
Summary: "Engaging text and colorful illustrations and photos teach
readers about sound"—Provided by publisher.
Audience: 4-8.
Audience: Grade K to 3.
Includes bibliographical references and index.
ISBN 978-1-4795-2187-6 (library binding)
ISBN 978-1-4795-2944-5 (paperback)
ISBN 978-1-4795-3323-7 (ebook pdf)
1. Sound—Juvenile literature. 2. Bats—Juvenile literature. 3. Dogs—
Juvenile literature. 4. Origami—Juvenile literature.
I. Title.
QC225.5.B733 2014
534—dc23   2013032499

Photo credits
Digital illustrations include royalty-free images from Shutterstock.

Capstone Studio: Karon Dubke, 22-23; Shutterstock: Blinka, 12-13
(sofa), Evgeniy Gorbunov, 10 (violin), Ivan Ponomarev, 10 (bass),
Melica, 10 (guitar), Robyn Mackenzie, 12-13 (frames)

Printed in the United States of America in Stevens Point, Wisconsin.
092013   007768WZS14

INTERNET SITES

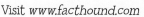

FactHound offers a safe, fun way to find Internet sites related to this book. All of the sites on FactHound have been researched by our staff.

Here's all you do:

Visit *www.facthound.com*

Type in this code: 9781479521876

Super-cool stuff!

Check out projects, games and lots more at **www.capstonekids.com**